BE FRUITFUL

The Call to Multiply What God Has Placed in Your Hands

Multiply, Fill the Earth, and Subdue

Dr. Tonia Ann Walker

COPYRIGHT PAGE

TABLE OF CONTENTS

DEDICATION PAGE

This book is dedicated to God, the Author of fruitfulness and the Giver of increase. May every seed planted through these pages bring forth fruit that remains, nourishing lives, restoring hope, and glorifying Him in every season.

"I am coaching, motivating, and educating others through my lived experiences."

Dr. Tonia Ann Walker

INTRODUCTION
BE FRUITFUL

Fruitfulness is not a suggestion in the Kingdom of God; it is a divine instruction.

From the beginning, God spoke increase into creation. He commanded life to grow, multiply, and produce after its kind. Fruitfulness was never meant to be forced or fabricated; it is the natural result of alignment with God, obedience to His voice, and connection to His purpose.

Yet many believers struggle with the idea of being fruitful. Not because they lack gifts, potential, or calling, but because they misunderstand the process. Fruit does not appear overnight. It develops in seasons. It requires proper planting, nurturing, pruning, and patience. What God has placed within you already carries the ability to produce, but it must be cultivated in the right environment.

This book is an invitation to examine your soil, your seeds, and your seasons. It will challenge you to recognize what God has entrusted to you, identify what may be hindering growth, and embrace the divine order that leads to increase. Fruitfulness is not about comparison or performance; it is about faithfulness and obedience.

As you journey through these pages, you will be encouraged to remain connected to the Source, trust God's timing, and believe that what He has spoken over your life will happen. When you abide in Him, fruit is inevitable.

This is your season to grow.
This is your season to multiply.
This is your season to **Be Fruitful**.

CHAPTER 1
RECOGNIZING YOUR TALENTS

Fruitfulness begins with recognition. Acknowledge what God has entrusted to you and refuse to let it remain unused. Before multiplication can occur, you must see your gifts, understand their purpose, and receive them as gifts from God.

God Has Entrusted You with More Than You Know

In the parable of the talents, Jesus told a story about a man preparing for a journey who entrusted his servants with his resources. The Lord gave each servant talents according to their ability. One received five, another two, and another one. No servants were given more than they could handle. Two servants immediately multiplied what they were given. One allowed fear to silence action and buried his gift in the ground. When the man returned, he said to the faithful servants:

"Well done, good and faithful servant.

You have been faithful over a little; I will place you over much."

But to the one who hid his gift, he gave a stern rebuke, and what he had was taken away. To everyone who uses what they have, more will be given. But to the one who does nothing, even what they have will be lost. Likewise, God has placcd gifts, opportunities, influence, and resources uniquely suited to you in your hands. – Matthew 25:14-30

Too often, people fail to be fruitful because they underestimate what they already have. You may think, *"I have only one talent, only a small gift, only a little opportunity."* But even a single talent, when placed in God's hands and acted upon in faith, can produce a harvest beyond imagination.

God does not call you to compare your talents with others. He calls you to steward what He has given to you. The servant with one talent could have doubled it if only he had believed it was enough.

Identifying Your Talents

To recognize your talents, ask yourself:

- What skills or gifts come naturally to me?

- Where do I see God's favor moving in my life?

- What opportunities repeatedly appear, nudging me toward action?

Talents are not always obvious. They may be:

- **Spiritual gifts**: teaching, prophecy, healing, and encouragement.

- **Natural abilities**: communication, leadership, and creativity.

- **Resources or connections**: money, influence, networks, and platforms.

- **Experiences**: trials, knowledge gained, and spiritual insights.

God often entrusts us with hidden treasures disguised as ordinary tools. Your ability to teach, listen, write, create, lead, or encourage is more powerful than you realize. The question is: will you see it, or will fear and doubt keep it buried?

Faith Awakens Fruitfulness

Recognizing your talents requires faith. Faith opens your eyes to the potential God has placed in you. Faith whispers, *"This is enough. God has given me exactly what I need."*

Faith moves you to action. Faith refuses to settle for mediocrity when God has called you to multiplication.

The servants who multiplied their talents did not wait for the Lord to return; they acted immediately, with courage and strategy. They invested what they had, and their faithfulness produced exponential results.

Your Assignment Today

Take a moment to list the talents God has entrusted to you. Write down every gift, skill, resource, and opportunity, even the small ones you think are insignificant. This is your starting point. The first step to fruitfulness is always recognition.

Remember: God has not given you talents to hide, hoard, or fearfully protect. He has given them to you to multiply, to expand, and to produce a harvest. Every day you delay in recognizing and acting on your gifts is a day the enemy hopes you remain stagnant.

You are not here by accident. You have been entrusted with treasures. Today is the day to open your eyes, step out in faith, and begin the journey to **be fruitful**.

CHAPTER 2

FEAR VS. FAITH: THE SIN OF INACTION

In the parable of the talents, one servant received a single talent. But instead of investing it, he buried it in the ground, saying, *"Lord, I knew you to be a hard man… and I was afraid."* His fear robbed him of fruitfulness.

Fear is the enemy of multiplication. Fear paralyzes potential, silences purpose, and causes even the smallest talent to remain dormant. God has given you gifts, opportunities, and influence, but if fear governs your actions, those gifts cannot grow.

Understanding Fear in Fruitfulness

Fear manifests in many ways:

- **Fear of failure**: "What if I try and it doesn't work?"

- **Fear of judgment**: "What will others think if I step out?"

- **Fear of inadequacy**: "I'm not skilled enough, talented enough, or ready."

The enemy whispers these lies because fear keeps you from producing fruit. Fear keeps you in the shadows, hiding your talents instead of investing in them. But faith moves against fear. Faith steps forward, even when the outcome is uncertain.

Faith is Action Amid Fear

Faith does not wait for fear to disappear. Faith acts despite fear. The servants who multiplied their talents did not have perfect conditions; they had courage and vision.

- Faith says, "I can do this because God equipped me."

- Faith says, "I will step out because the Lord has called me."

- Faith says, "I trust the increase to God, not my limitations."

When you act in faith, God not only multiplies your efforts but also your abilities.

Excuses Are the Enemy of Fruitfulness

Notice that the unfruitful servant did not merely fail; he excused his inaction. Excuses are the masks of fear:

- "I don't have enough resources."

- "I'm not ready yet."

- "Someone else can do it better."

Excuses sound reasonable, but they kill potential. God is not impressed by excuses; He is pleased by faithfulness. Every day you postpone stepping out in faith is another day you risk the talents He entrusted to you being wasted.

Overcoming Fear with Bold Action

Here's how to replace fear with faith and start producing fruit:

1. **Identify the fear:** Write down what is holding you back.

2. **Counter it with God's Word:** For every fear, declare a truth from Scripture.

3. **Take a small step in obedience:** Action produces momentum. You don't have to do everything at once, start.

4. **Accountability:** Surround yourself with those who encourage faith-filled action.

5. **Celebrate victories:** Every step forward is a seed sown for greater multiplication.

Your Assignment Today

Ask yourself: *What talent am I hiding because of fear? What opportunity am I avoiding because of doubt?*

Then take one bold action, no matter how small, to invest that talent. Write, speak, teach, create, serve, whatever your gift may be. Fear will resist, but faith will obey.

Remember: God rewards action. He honors courage. He multiplies the faithfulness of those who refuse to be paralyzed. The servant who buried his talent was called wicked and lazy, but the faithful servants were called good and faithful.

Do not let fear rob you of your inheritance. Step forward. Act boldly. Trust God. And begin the journey to be fruitful.

CHAPTER 3
INVESTMENT AND MULTIPLICATION

Fruitfulness is not accidental. It requires intentional investment, time, energy, resources, and faith poured into the gifts God has entrusted to you. The parable of the talents teaches that God expects growth. He expects His servants to multiply what He has given them, not simply preserve it.

The Principle of Spiritual Investment

Every talent, gift, or opportunity is like a seed. A seed left in the hand or buried in the ground produces nothing. A seed sown in the right environment, nurtured with care, produces a harvest.

God's kingdom operates on a principle of multiplication.

- **Spiritual talents** multiply through service, prayer, and obedience.

- **Natural abilities** multiply through practice, discipline, and mentorship.

- **Resources** multiply when invested wisely, not hoarded.

Multiplication does not require a perfect plan or ideal circumstances; it requires faithful action. The servants who doubled their talents acted with diligence and creativity, trusting that God would honor their efforts.

Investing Your Talents

Here's how to begin:

1. **Use What You Have Right Now:**
   You don't need to wait until you feel fully equipped. God multiplies faithful beginnings.

   - Write that book.
   - Start that ministry.
   - Begin mentoring or teaching.

2. **Apply Your Skills and Gifts:**
   Every gift has a purpose. Identify where your talents meet the needs of others. Serving others is the primary soil in which fruitfulness grows.

3. **Take Calculated Risks:**
   Investment requires courage. The servant who hid his talent feared risk, but growth always involves stepping out of your comfort zone. Bold action produces harvest.

4. **Reinvest the Returns:**
   When God blesses your efforts, do not stop. Multiply again. Reinvest your profits, your influence, and your time. Fruitfulness grows exponentially when fed with persistence and faith.

The Role of Faith in Multiplication

Faith is the engine of multiplication. Without faith, no effort yields lasting fruit. Faith leads you to act when results are unseen. Faith trusts God to take small efforts and make them great.

- Faith does not complain: *"I don't have enough."*

- Faith does not compare: *"Someone else is better equipped."*

- Faith acts: *"I will serve, sow, and invest, trusting God for increase."*

Practical Steps to Multiply Your Talents

- **Create a plan:** Map out how you will use your talents in the next 30, 60, and 90 days.

- **Measure results:** Track progress. Celebrate every increase, no matter how small.

- **Seek mentorship:** Learn from those who have successfully multiplied their gifts.

- **Give back:** Teaching, serving, and mentoring others multiplies fruitfulness beyond personal gain.

Your Assignment Today

Take one talent God has given you and invest it this week. It can be as simple as:

- Teaching someone a skill you excel at.

- Using your influence to open a door for someone else.

- Offering your time to serve in your community or ministry.

Do not bury your talent in fear, in hesitation, or in waiting for "the right time." The right time is now. Multiply what God has entrusted to you and watch as your small efforts become a harvest beyond your imagination.

CHAPTER 4
THE REWARD OF FAITHFULNESS

"Well done, good and faithful servant; you have been faithful over a few things, I will make you ruler over many things. Enter the joy of your Lord." – Matthew 25:23

Faithfulness produces fruit, and fruitfulness produces reward. The parable of the talents reveals that God does not overlook diligence, obedience, or courage. Every step you take to invest your gifts, multiply your talent, and walk in obedience is noticed and honored by God.

The Nature of God's Reward

God's reward for faithfulness is twofold:

1. **Spiritual Reward:**

    - Peace, joy, and confidence in your purpose.

    - Growth in character, wisdom, and spiritual maturity.

    - A deeper intimacy with God as He entrusts you with greater responsibility.

2. **Practical Reward:**

    - Increased influence in your relationships, community, or workplace.

    - Favor and opportunities that align with your gifts.

    - Material and financial increase, often as a natural consequence of faithful stewardship.

Faithfulness is never wasted. Even small acts of obedience, praying for someone, mentoring a younger believer, or words of encouragement, are investments in God's kingdom that yield eternal dividends.

Faithfulness Multiplies Trust

The more faithful you are with little, the more God entrusts you with much. The parable emphasizes that growth is sequential:

- Small acts of obedience lead to larger assignments.

- Consistency in faithfulness attracts trust from God and others.

- Multiplication happens when you honor the little things, knowing God sees and rewards every effort.

Faithfulness also builds credibility. Just as the Lord entrusted more to the diligent servants, God entrusts greater resources, influence, and opportunities to those who consistently invest and act with integrity.

The Joy of the Lord

The ultimate reward is relational and eternal: joy in the Lord's presence. God's pleasure is not merely in your productivity but in your faithful heart, your courage, and your willingness to act in alignment with His will.

This joy is both present and eternal:

- Present, as you experience fulfillment, peace, and purpose in this life.

- Eternal, as your faithfulness contributes to your inheritance in God's kingdom.

Faithfulness Requires Perseverance

Rewards are not always immediate. Sometimes the harvest takes seasons to appear. The key is perseverance. Continue sowing, investing, and multiplying, even when results seem slow or unseen. God honors those who endure.

Your Assignment Today

Reflect on your recent acts of faithfulness. Ask yourself:

- Have I been consistent in investing my talents?

- Have I taken bold action, even when it felt risky?

- Am I faithfully serving God and others with the gifts He entrusted to me?

Then, take one more step of faithfulness today:

- Make that call, share that teaching, complete that project, mentor someone.

- Remember, God multiplies faithfulness into fruitfulness, and fruitfulness into reward.

Do not measure your reward by human standards. God's kingdom operates on a principle of divine multiplication and eternal significance.

Step forward in faithfulness, and the Lord will say,

"Well done, good and faithful servant."

CHAPTER 5
LESSONS FROM THE UNFRUITFUL SERVANT

In the parable of the talents, one servant received a single talent and buried it in the ground. He did not invest, multiply, or act. When the leader returned, he was called wicked and lazy. This servant teaches us a critical lesson: fruitlessness is costly.

Why Talents Remain Dormant

There are key reasons why God's gifts remain unfruitful in people's lives:

1. **Fear of Failure:**
   Fear is a thief. The unfruitful servant feared the Lord's expectations, believing that any misstep would bring judgment. Many believers hide their gifts because they fear failure, criticism, or disappointment.

2. **Lack of Faith:**
   Faith is the engine of fruitfulness. Without trust in God's provision and guidance, talents remain buried. Doubt convinces us that our efforts are too small to matter.

3. **Procrastination:**
   The enemy often uses delays to paralyze action. Waiting for the "perfect moment" or "more resources" can indefinitely prevent growth.

4. **Comparison:**
   Measuring your talents against others leads to discouragement or jealousy. Every servant received

talents according to ability; comparison is not the standard.

5. **Disobedience:**
   The unfruitful servant disobeyed by not using the talent entrusted to him. Fruitfulness requires action. Spiritual gifts, resources, and opportunities left unused are a form of disobedience.

The Cost of Fruitlessness

Fruitlessness has consequences:

- **Spiritual Loss**: You miss God's blessing and the joy of fulfilling your purpose.

- **Opportunity Lost**: Others may not receive the impact you were meant to deliver.

- **Divine Rebuke**: The parable labels unfruitful action as wicked and lazy. God expects diligence, initiative, and obedience.

Turning Dormancy into Multiplication

Even if you've been unfruitful, God's grace allows a fresh start. The keys are recognition, repentance, and action:

1. **Recognize** areas where you've been inactive or hiding your talents.

2. **Repent** of fear, laziness, or excuses that have held you back.

3. **Act** immediately, invest, serve, teach, or create, using what God has entrusted to you.

Overcoming the Traps of Inaction

- **Replace fear with faith**: Declare God's promises over your life and talents.

- **Break procrastination cycles**: Commit to one actionable step each day.

- **Stop comparing**: Focus on your unique gifts and opportunities.

- **Embrace obedience**: Do what God asks, even if the results are unseen at first.

Your Assignment Today

Identify one talent, gift, or opportunity that you've been hiding or neglecting. Ask yourself:

- What fear or excuse has kept me from using it?

- How can I take one step today to invest it?

Then, take that step. Even a small act of obedience begins a chain reaction of multiplication. Remember: God does not reward hidden potential; He rewards faithful action.

Your gifts are too valuable to remain dormant. The world needs your fruit. Do not allow fear, doubt, or delay to rob you of your destiny. Step into action and **be fruitful**.

CHAPTER 6
STRATEGIES FOR DAILY FRUITFULNESS

Fruitfulness is not a one-time event; it is a lifestyle. Just as a tree produces fruit season after season, a believer who seeks to be fruitful must cultivate habits, disciplines, and strategies that lead to consistent multiplication.

1. Prioritize Your Talents Daily:

Every day, make a conscious choice to invest in your gifts. This means:

- Allocating time to develop your skills.

- Using your spiritual gifts to serve others.

- Identifying opportunities to influence, teach, or mentor.

Small, consistent actions accumulate over time. A single act may seem insignificant, but repeated daily, it produces exponential results.

2. Set Clear Goals for Multiplication:

Fruitfulness requires intentionality. Ask yourself:

- What do I want to multiply in the next 30 days?

- What talents or resources can I sow to see growth?

- How will I measure progress and celebrate milestones?

Write down your goals and break them into actionable steps. Faith without action remains dormant; clarity without execution yields no fruit.

3. Engage in Spiritual Discipline:

Spiritual practices create fertile ground for your talents to flourish. Include:

- **Prayer**: Seek God's guidance on where and how to invest your talents.

- **Study of Scripture**: Understand God's principles for multiplication.

- **Fasting and Reflection**: Remove distractions and align with God's purpose.

The more you stay connected to the source, the greater the fruitfulness will be.

4. Take Calculated Risks:

God multiplies bold action. Don't wait for the perfect moment. Invest what you have now, even if the outcome is uncertain. Bold steps often lead to breakthroughs that cautious planning alone cannot achieve.

5. Reinvest Your Fruit:

As your efforts begin to yield results, reinvest what you have gained:

- Teach and mentor others using your skills.

- Expand your influence through service and leadership.

- Use financial or material gains to create new opportunities.

Multiplication is not linear; it is expansive. One faithful investment can lead to multiple harvests when reinvested wisely.

6. Maintain Accountability:

Fruitfulness thrives in community. Seek mentors, partners, or accountability partners who will:

- Encourage your growth.
- Hold you accountable for action.
- Celebrate your victories with you.

Collaboration and accountability prevent stagnation; ensure that your talents are not wasted.

7. Reflect and Adjust Regularly:

Regular reflection ensures that your efforts are aligned with God's purpose. Ask yourself:

- Which actions are producing fruit?
- Where am I wasting energy on unproductive tasks?
- How can I adjust my strategy to maximize impact?

Reflection turns experience into wisdom and allows multiplication over time.

Your Assignment Today:

Choose one talent or resource you will invest consistently every day this week. Set a goal, act, and schedule a daily reflection to track progress.

Remember: Fruitfulness is a daily commitment, not a one-time achievement. God has entrusted you with talents, and He expects a return on them. When you invest intentionally, act boldly, and stay disciplined, your life becomes a living testimony of multiplication and impact.

CHAPTER 7
LEGACY OF FRUITFULNESS

Fruitfulness is not just about the harvest you see today; it is about the impact you leave for tomorrow. God's principle of multiplication extends beyond your lifetime. The talents He entrusts to you are meant to produce a legacy that touches generations.

The Eternal Perspective of Fruitfulness

The parable of the talents reminds us that God evaluates not only what we do with what we have but also the lasting impact of our faithfulness. Every act of investment, service, teaching, and multiplication contributes to a spiritual and practical legacy.

Legacy is not measured solely in wealth or influence; it is measured by:

- **Lives transformed** through your service and mentorship.

- **Faith is instilled** in others who follow your example.

- **Kingdom expansion** through obedience and multiplication of your gifts.

When you live fruitfully, you are creating a harvest that blesses generations.

Influence Through Relationships

Your talents and resources are multiplied when shared with others. Mentoring, teaching, and guiding others are ways to ensure that your impact continues. Ask yourself:

- Who can I mentor or teach today?

- Who will benefit from the talents God has entrusted to me?

- How can I leave a legacy of faith, courage, and fruitfulness?

Your influence creates a chain reaction. Those you empower today become the leaders, teachers, and faithful stewards of tomorrow.

Stewardship and Inheritance

Fruitfulness is an act of stewardship. God entrusts resources, gifts, and opportunities to each believer with the expectation of increase. Stewardship extends to how your legacy is handed down:

- Financial resources and material blessings can create opportunities for others.

- Wisdom, experience, and faithfulness leave a spiritual inheritance.

- Generational fruitfulness transforms families, communities, and nations.

Lessons from the Servants

The servants who multiplied their talents received commendation and greater responsibility. Their legacy was not just the immediate reward; it was the expansion of God's kingdom through their faithfulness.

The unfruitful servant left nothing behind. Fear, inaction, and excuses cost him his legacy. Your choice today determines not only your harvest but also the seed you plant for future generations.

Your Assignment Today

Consider the impact of your faithfulness beyond yourself. Ask:

- How will my actions today influence those around me?

- What can I invest now to ensure my legacy of fruitfulness endures?

- Who needs the multiplication of my talents, resources, or gifts?

Begin today to sow seeds that will grow long after you are gone. Be intentional, be bold, and be faithful. Your life is meant to produce fruit, fruit that lasts, fruit that blesses, fruit that carries the mark of God's kingdom across generations.

Remember: True fruitfulness is never short-term, echoing into eternity.

CHAPTER 8
CONCLUSION:
YOUR TALENTS ARE NOT YOURS

Everything you have, your gifts, talents, resources, and opportunities, has been entrusted to you by God. They are not yours to hoard, hide, or fearfully protect. They are His, and He expects fruitfulness.

The parable of the talents is a divine reminder: God measures not only what we receive but what we do with it. Faithfulness, diligence, courage, and obedience produce multiplication. Fear, inaction, and excuses produce nothing.

Step Into Your Divine Assignment

God has entrusted you with specific abilities and opportunities tailored for you. They are unique, irreplaceable, and powerful. Ask yourself:

- Am I acting boldly with what God has entrusted to me?

- Am I faithfully investing my talents for His kingdom?

- Am I willing to take risks, step out in faith, and trust God for multiplication?

The Cost of Inaction

Remember the unfruitful servant. Fear, comparison, and hesitation cost him not only reward but also purpose. Hiding your talents is a spiritual loss, not just for you, but for those God intended you to impact.

The Reward of Faithfulness

Faithfulness brings spiritual and eternal reward. Every step of obedience multiplies your influence, produces impact, and leaves a legacy. The faithful servant is called faithful, invited into joy, honor, and expanded responsibility.

A Call to Action

- **Recognize** the talents God has entrusted to you.

- **Act boldly** in faith, even in the face of fear.

- **Invest and multiply** your gifts consistently.

- **Build a legacy** that blesses generations.

Your life is meant to be fruitful, not just for personal gain, but to advance God's kingdom. Every talent, every opportunity, every gift is a seed waiting to produce a harvest.

Do not delay. Do not hide. Do not underestimate what God has entrusted to you.
Step into faith, take bold action, and live a life of multiplication.

The world is waiting for the fruit God has placed in your hands.

Be courageous.

Be obedient.

Be faithful.

And **Be Fruitful.**

CHAPTER 9
I AM BEARING FRUIT THAT REMAINS

I am expanding my territory through writing books, journals, and educating others. With every page I write and every life I touch, I advance the purpose God has placed within me. I am not hiding what He entrusted to me; I am multiplying it.

I am reminded of the Parable of the Talents, where the servant who stewarded what he was given received an increase. As Scripture declares:

"For to everyone who has, more will be given, and he will have abundance. Whoever does not have, even what he has, will be taken from him."
— *Matthew 25:29 (NIV)*

This truth is powerful. I once heard a well-known actress share that when she had nothing, no one offered help. Yet once she became successful, opportunities and support increased, even when she no longer needed them. **Such is the principle: to those who have, more is given.**

I choose multiplication.
I choose stewardship.
I choose to increase.

I am growing in every area of my life, career, family, love, health, and well-being. I am becoming whole, aligned, and strengthened from the inside out. What God is cultivating within me is now bearing visible fruit.

This is a season of expansion and divine increase. Multiplication is my portion. Opportunities are growing. Influence is widening.

Impact is deepening. What I place in God's hands cannot remain small.

I am fruitful. I am multiplying. I am walking boldly in purpose.

NEXT STEPS

Thank you for reading. *Be Fruitful, Multiply, Fill the Earth, and Subdue it! "This is enough. God has given me exactly what I need."*

I hope this book has encouraged you, reminded you of your purpose, and inspired you to walk boldly into the blessings God has prepared just for you.

To help you further, look for the accompanying *Journal: Be Fruitful.* It is designed to guide your reflections, prayers, and declarations as you apply the lessons from this book.

I'd love to hear from you! Share your thoughts, breakthroughs, or questions; your story might inspire someone else.

Email: thecoachingcreator@gmail.com
Website: www.thecoachingcreator.com

Keep moving in faith, trusting God's timing, and stepping fully into the life He has called you to. The best is still ahead!

With gratitude and encouragement,

Dr. Tonia Ann Walker